birds were also easy to shoot because they flew so
close together. By the 1870s, thousands of people
hunted them full time. It seemed that there would
always be great flocks of the birds. Yet by the
early 1900s, the last wild passenger pigeon had
disappeared. Rewards of up to $5,000 were offered to
anyone who could find a nesting pair. But no one was
able to claim the rewards. The last known passenger
pigeons were two males and a female named Martha.
They lived at the Cincinnati Zoo, in Ohio. The two males
died first. Martha lived on for four more years. She died
on September 1, 1914. With her death, the passenger
pigeon became extinct.

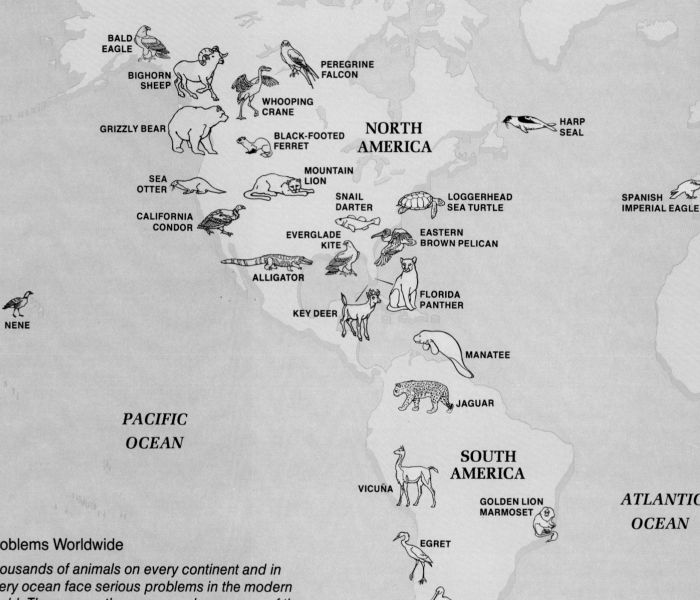

POLAR BEAR

BALD EAGLE

BIGHORN SHEEP

WHOOPING CRANE

PEREGRINE FALCON

GRIZZLY BEAR

BLACK-FOOTED FERRET

NORTH AMERICA

HARP SEAL

SEA OTTER

MOUNTAIN LION

SNAIL DARTER

LOGGERHEAD SEA TURTLE

SPANISH IMPERIAL EAGLE

CALIFORNIA CONDOR

EVERGLADE KITE

EASTERN BROWN PELICAN

ALLIGATOR

FLORIDA PANTHER

NENE

KEY DEER

MANATEE

JAGUAR

PACIFIC OCEAN

SOUTH AMERICA

VICUÑA

GOLDEN LION MARMOSET

ATLANTIC OCEAN

EGRET

ROSEATE SPOONBILL

Problems Worldwide

Thousands of animals on every continent and in every ocean face serious problems in the modern world. The map on these pages shows many of the animals pictured elsewhere in this book and areas where they live. Some, such as the wolf, live in more than one part of the world. Others, such as Florida's Everglade kite, live only in one small area. Almost everywhere, animals suffer from the loss of their homes, from hunting, or from poisoning and pollution. Many animals suffer from more than one of these problems in their struggle to survive.

8

ANTARCTICA PENGUIN

EUROPE

EUROPEAN
WHITE STORK

WOLF

ASIA

PACIFIC
OCEAN

AFRICA

CHEETAH

GIRAFFE

TIGER

RHESUS
MONKEY

AFRICAN
ELEPHANT

MOUNTAIN
GORILLA

BLACK
RHINOCEROS

RADIATED
TORTOISE

ORANGUTAN

INDIAN
OCEAN

AUSTRALIA

KOALA

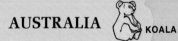
HUMPBACK
WHALE

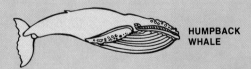

(Continued from page 6) few of these species and areas where they live. Almost all animals that are in danger suffer from problems caused by people. Some of the problems that people cause are unintentional. Among these is the greatest threat that many animals face—the loss of a place to live.

Homes Lost

Humans can adjust to living almost anywhere. But many animals can live only in certain areas. The place where an animal naturally lives is called its habitat. A habitat may be as large as a forest that stretches for miles or as small as a tiny pond. Animals depend on their habitats for their survival. There, they find food and raise their young.

Through the centuries, many of the places where animals once lived have been taken over by humans. As the human population has increased, people have needed more and more land to make room for growing cities and new farms.

Building even one new house can destroy the habitat of a small animal, such as an insect or a mouse. Expanding cities and new farms can destroy the habitat of an entire species. If the species cannot find another place where it is able to live, it cannot survive.

Many times, people have destroyed the homes of animals they love without realizing it. This has happened to the white stork—one of the most popular birds in Europe. Each spring, Europeans look forward to the return of the storks from their wintering grounds in Africa. The tall, graceful birds are a welcome sight as they glide in for a landing with their broad wings outstretched.

For hundreds of years, white storks have built their large nests on the chimneys and rooftops of buildings. But some of the old buildings in Europe have been torn down. And few new buildings provide the right kind of nesting sites. So the storks have fewer places to live.

In addition to having fewer nesting places, the storks have fewer places where they can find food. Much of the countryside where the storks once found fish and other small animals to eat has now been taken over to make room for more buildings and roads.

The storks cannot continue to live in areas where they can no longer find food or places to build their nests. In some

Perched high on a chimney-top nest, a white stork in northeastern France watches over its young. The white stork is one of the favorite birds of many Europeans. A stork on the roof is believed to bring good luck. Some people build false chimneys on their roofs, or put up tall platforms where the storks can build their nests. But white storks today still have fewer places to nest than they once had. They also have fewer areas in which to find food.

parts of Switzerland, Holland, Belgium, and Denmark, the birds have lost so much of their habitat that they have completely disappeared.

Dangers of Overhunting

Pressure from hunting is another problem that threatens wildlife. People have always hunted animals. Before they began to raise animals for food, humans depended on the meat of wild animals. Some people still do.

But today, most animals are hunted for other reasons. Huge profits are made by selling live animals and animal products. Sometimes, an entire animal is used to make a variety of products. The whale is one example.

Some whales are among the biggest animals that have ever lived. Blue whales are larger than the huge dinosaurs that once roamed the earth. Blue whales can weigh nearly 200 tons (180 t)*—as much as 30 African elephants.

Before the days of electricity, people used oil lamps to light their homes. Whales were the main source of oil for those lamps. Men went to sea in sailing ships to search the oceans of the world for whales. Excited cries went up whenever a crew member spotted a whale.

But whale oil is no longer needed for lamps. Today, people hunt whales for other reasons. In some countries, many products are made from these huge mammals. The products include pet food, margarine, soap, and crayons. Whale teeth are sometimes used to make piano keys. Even the whale's blood is used—to make products such as fertilizer and glue. And people in some countries eat the meat of whales.

Only a few nations still have fleets of whaling ships. But over the years, better and faster ships and improved weapons have made it easier to find and kill whales. Large numbers can be killed by the few whalers who still hunt them.

Many nations want to limit the number of whales killed. These nations have agreed that the hunting of certain kinds of whales should end. They have also agreed that fewer of the kinds of whales still hunted should be killed.

Each year, these countries set a limit on the number of whales that can be legally killed. The yearly limit set for 1980 was 15,835. But some countries pay no attention to such limits. They kill even those whales in danger of extinction.   11

*Metric figures in this book are given in round numbers.

Female white stork in Milicz, Poland, grooms her feathers (above). Her mate sits on the eggs in their nest. The birds take turns sitting on the eggs. White storks travel as far as 14,000 miles (22,500 km) round trip on their yearly migrations. The map at left shows their routes. Storks spend the winters in several parts of Africa. Each spring, they return to Europe, often to the same nests.

Giants With Big Problems

Baby humpback whale swims with its mother. Humpbacks like these can grow to be more than 40 feet (12 m) long and weigh 40 tons (36 t). Despite the fact that humpbacks have been protected by an international agreement since 1966, their numbers are not increasing. Some scientists think there may already be too few of the whales left for the species to survive. Other kinds of whales are also in danger. Hunters kill thousands of whales each year.

Poisoning and Pollution

A major problem that animals in many parts of the world face is the danger of being harmed by poisonous chemicals introduced into their environments. At times, such chemicals may be introduced on purpose. Some animals, such as the wolf and the coyote, are poisoned intentionally. These animals are considered to be pests by some people because they sometimes kill livestock, such as sheep or cattle.

At other times, chemicals may be introduced into an animal's environment unintentionally, in the form of pollution. To help protect their crops, farmers often use chemicals to kill harmful insects. These same chemicals can harm other animals that accidentally come in contact with them. And thousands of factories release chemicals into the air and into streams and oceans. These chemicals can also harm animals.

One animal that has been affected by pollution is the bald eagle—the great bird that symbolizes the United States. Most people have probably never seen a bald eagle in the wild. The 14 bald eagle was a common sight when it became America's

national bird in 1782. But now, chemicals in some of the food the eagles eat have caused them to produce fewer young. As a result, the birds have disappeared from many states.

Working To Save Animals

Today, scientists and government officials around the world are trying to find solutions to the many problems that animals face. One big step forward came in America in 1973. In that year, the U. S. Congress passed the Endangered Species Act. This act helps protect animals that are in danger of extinction. Such animals are said to be "endangered." The act also helps protect "threatened" animals—those that aren't yet endangered but that do face serious threats to their survival.

Many private national and international organizations are also trying to help animals survive. Some groups hope to stop the hunting of certain kinds of animals. Others are working to protect existing animal habitats, or to set aside special areas where wildlife can live.

But even governments face difficult problems in trying to save animals. One problem is that not everyone agrees on which animals should be protected. Different nations have different laws. In the United States, laws vary from state to state. Sometimes an animal may be protected in one area and legally hunted in another. The alligator is an example.

Scientists say that alligators have been on earth for millions of years. Today, in the United States, the bellow of the alligator is heard in ten southern states. People kill alligators for their valuable hides. Over the years, they killed so many in the U. S. that in the 1960s, all alligator hunting was banned. Since then, the number of alligators has increased.

Because of this increase, the State of Louisiana now allows limited alligator hunting. Officials there say that even though alligators are endangered in many areas, they are not endangered in parts of their state. Other people say that alligators should be protected everywhere they live.

Helping alligators and other animals is not always an easy job. But one thing is clear—more and more animals will need help if they are to survive. Humans share the earth with animals. It is up to people to make sure that future generations will be able to hear the bellow of the alligator and the howl of the wolf.

Alligator in a Florida wildlife refuge lies in a bed of water lettuce (below). Millions of alligators were killed in the United States between the early 1800s and the 1960s. Although alligator hunting is banned in most states, laws vary. Hunters in Louisiana (right) lift a legally killed alligator into their boat.

Rolled-up alligator hides lie ready for sale after a hunt in Louisiana. Factories will use the hides to make shoes, belts, wallets, and purses.

One Area, Many Problems

The State of Florida is an example of an area where nature has been thrown out of balance by the activities of people. Many people have moved to Florida in recent years because of the area's beauty and warm climate. Builders have drained swamps, lakes, and marshes to make room for construction. These areas, called wetlands, are among the most delicate of all environments in North America. They are home to many kinds of animals. As people clear these areas, the homes of animals and the food the areas provide disappear. Other problems exist in Florida. Rare animals that are protected by law are sometimes illegally killed by hunters. Some animals are accidentally harmed by humans who simply live too close to them. These two pages and the following four show a few of Florida's endangered animals.

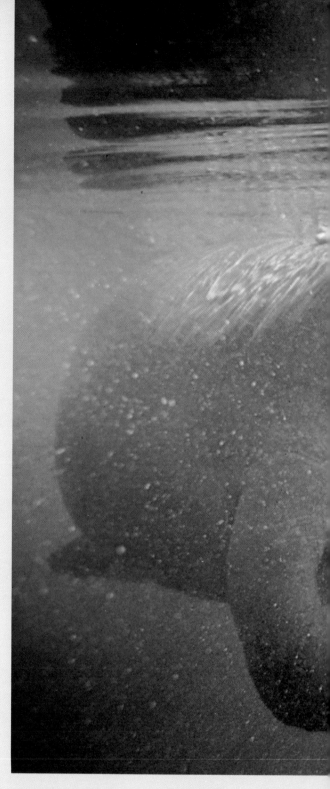

Manatees (left, inside circle) swim in a Florida canal. Once numerous, manatees are now disappearing. Only about a thousand are left in Florida's waters.

Two divers play with a gentle manatee (above). Manatees, which weigh up to 2,000 pounds (900 kg), live along Florida's coast and in its waterways, often in popular boating areas. Boat propellers can injure or kill the slow-moving creatures. A sign (right) warns boaters they are in an area where manatees live.

Vanishing Bird

Everglade kite (left) glides over a marshy lake. Once found in many southern Florida marshes, Everglade kites are now among the rarest birds in North America. A few survive in refuges such as the one above. Here, wildlife warden Roderick Chandler puts a kite nest with eggs inside a wire frame. The frame is left in place to hold the fragile nest together.

Returning to its nest, an Everglade kite brings a snail to its chicks (above). Kites are a type of hawk. They live in marshy areas because their only food source, the apple snail (right), is found nowhere else. When wetlands are drained by builders, the apple snail disappears. And so do Everglade kites. Some experts believe the kite will become extinct in just a few more years, as people continue to drain Florida wetlands. Probably no more than a hundred Everglade kites still exist.

Hunted Animals

THE LAST OF THE TOY DEER OF THE FLORIDA KEYS

Some of Florida's animals have been hunted nearly to extinction. Key deer (left) live on the Florida Keys, small islands off the southern tip of the state. The drawing above, done in 1934, shows how hunters used dogs to chase the tiny deer into the water. Once in the water, the deer were easy to shoot. About 30 years ago, Glenn Allen, an 11-year-old from Miami, Florida, learned that just a few Key deer were left. He wanted to save the animals. Glenn, his classmates, and local Boy Scouts all wrote letters to newspapers and lawmakers. Glenn even wrote to the President of the United States. Other people who heard about the Key deer also wrote letters. Because so many people wanted to save the deer, the federal government created a wildlife refuge for them in 1954. Now the Key deer population is slowly increasing. Another endangered animal, the Florida panther (right) lives in the southern part of the state. Although panthers are protected by law, some people still shoot them. There may be no more than 50 of the cats alive today. Experts fear the Florida panther will become extinct in only a few more years.

African elephants roam inside Kenya's Amboseli National Park. In many places, elephants and other wild animals are losing their homes to the growing human population. To help animals survive in a changing world, national parks and other areas are being set aside for their protection.

2
Disappearing Homes

Giraffes, the world's tallest animals, browse in a national park in Kenya. Not far away, skyscrapers in the spreading city of Nairobi occupy an area where animals once lived.

On a hot, dusty plain in Africa, a mother elephant curls her trunk around her newborn baby. Gently, she lifts the 250-pound (115 kg) calf, helping it to stay up on its wobbly legs. Other elephants from the same herd stand nearby.

The baby elephant begins to feed on its mother's milk. Later, when this elephant grows up, it will need a large area in which to roam to find enough food. Adult elephants eat about 300 pounds (135 kg) of plants daily. Elephants may walk 20 to 30 miles (30-50 km) in a day searching for water and food.

While feeding, elephants may strip the bark from trees. Or they may push over trees and nibble on the roots and leaves. Feeding elephants sometimes leave a wide trail of uprooted trees behind them. Once, elephant herds roamed nearly all of Africa. But much of their range has been taken over by people. Each year, thousands of wilderness acres 25 in Africa are taken over for growing cities and new farms.

Many elephants now live within the boundaries of national parks. When the huge animals are crowded together inside parks, they often have a hard time finding enough food. Herds of elephants sometimes wander outside the parks as they search for food. They often stray onto farms and destroy crops. Rangers must sometimes use helicopters to drive the herds back into the parks.

Elephants in Africa face a problem that many animals throughout the world now face—how to survive with less and less land on which to live.

Smaller Homes, Less Food

While elephants need a certain amount of land to roam if they are to find enough plants to eat, meat-eaters, such as cheetahs, need a certain amount of space to find enough prey. A mother cheetah in Africa may wander for miles each day hunting for prey. Often, she must feed two or three hungry cubs.

Every day, a mother cheetah returns to her cubs by sunset. During the daylight hours, the cubs hide from animals that might kill them for food. Cheetah cubs depend on their mother until they are a year old. Throughout that time, the mother has no help in finding food. Cheetahs do not live and hunt in large groups as some animals do.

Cheetahs can run faster than any other animal—more than 70 miles (115 km) an hour over short distances. Because of their speed, they are able to run down prey they surprise. But as Africa's wilderness grows smaller, there is less prey for cheetahs to hunt. Sometimes the cats kill cattle or sheep for food. Ranchers then shoot or trap the cheetahs as pests.

Cheetahs and elephants are not the only African animals that have suffered because they are losing their homes. Experts believe the number of wild animals now in Africa is only about one tenth of what it was in 1900. Many animals were unable to survive because they no longer had large enough areas in which to live and find food.

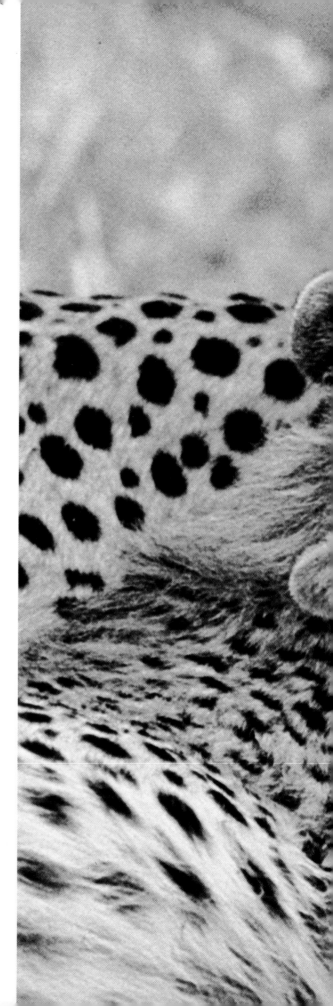

Cheetah cub in Africa licks its mother's face. Cheetahs can run fast enough to catch antelopes and other animals. But the cats need a large territory to find enough prey.

Adult mountain gorilla (left) roams through a forest in its central African home. Mountain gorillas are larger than any other kind of ape. A male may weigh up to 400 pounds (180 kg) and stand six feet (185 cm) tall. The gorillas live in small groups. Older gorillas, whose backs have turned silver or gray with age, lead the groups. Over the years, many parts of the mountain gorilla's habitat have been taken over by humans.

Close-up look at scientist Dian Fossey's face seems to fascinate a baby mountain gorilla (right). Dr. Fossey's studies of the gorillas have helped people learn more about them. Some people think that gorillas, such as the male below, are ferocious. But experts have found they are actually gentle and shy. Gorillas often run away when they see a human.

Help Through Understanding

Scientists often study wild animals so they will have a better idea of how to protect them and help them increase in number. The scientists find out what the animals eat, how they raise their young, and how much land they need to live on.

One scientist, Dr. Dian Fossey, has spent more than ten years studying mountain gorillas in central Africa. The shy, gentle animals are found mostly in protected forest areas called reserves.

Even though these areas are protected, mountain gorillas still suffer from the loss of their homes. Local people cut down the trees in the forests where the gorillas live. And herders bring their cattle into the forests to graze. Some people even shoot the gorillas, or capture young ones and sell them to animal exporters.

Dr. Fossey has found that the apes cannot share their territory with humans and survive. There were about a thousand mountain gorillas in 1971. Because much of the animals' habitat has been taken over by people, the number of gorillas has decreased to about 500.

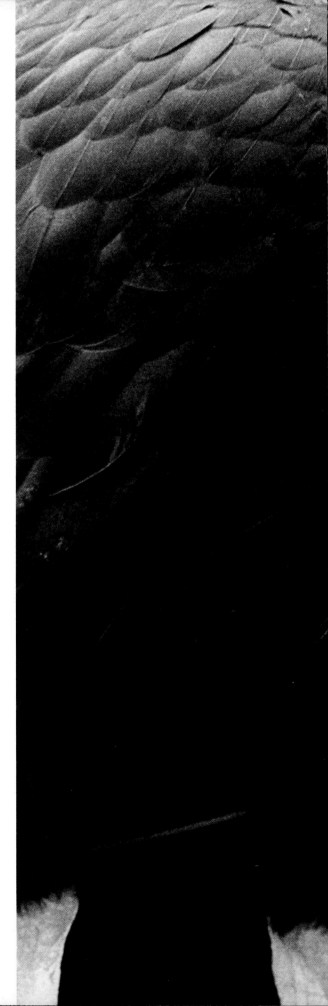

California's Vanishing Condors

Just as Dr. Dian Fossey is studying Africa's mountain gorillas, scientists, government officials, and private citizens in the United States are studying the California condor. They hope to learn what can be done to save this bird.

Scientists say condors date back more than a million years—to the time of the saber-toothed tiger. When Europeans first explored the Pacific coast, condors ranged from southern Canada to northern Mexico. The condor's range has now shrunk to a small area in central and southern California. The condors live in wildlife refuges and on private land.

At one time, there were hundreds of condors. As they searched for food, the birds soared on wings measuring nine feet (275 cm) from tip to tip. They sometimes flew as far as a hundred miles (160 km) from their homes looking for food. Now there are only about 30 condors left. And few of these are

California condor searches the countryside for dead animals to eat. Its mate sits near the pair's cliffside nest. The number of condors is declining. A pair of condors produces just one egg every two years, and only a few pairs are still breeding. Scientists hope to save condors by breeding them in captivity.

30

Bald head, sharp beak, and black feathers give the California condor a fierce look. A kind of vulture, the California condor is one of North America's most endangered birds.

Grizzly bear plods through snow in Mt. McKinley National Park, in Alaska. Grizzlies sleep for long periods in winter. They get up occasionally to search for food.

producing young. Although condors have other problems, the birds have disappeared mainly because of a loss of habitat. Towns and farms now cover much of the area where the birds once lived and found food. And some scientists think the noise from machinery may upset the shy condors.

Some experts believe California condors cannot survive without help. These people want to capture condors and breed them in captivity. They plan to release the birds in the wild when they are old enough to survive on their own. The experts believe the chances of successful breeding are good. Condors of other species have mated in captivity.

Humans in Wilderness Areas

Many North American animals besides the condor have lost their homes. Grizzly bears, for example, once lived in the western mountains and plains from Alaska to Mexico. As the West was settled, much of the bears' territory was taken over by humans. People shot the grizzlies for their warm fur. They also killed grizzlies because they were afraid of them, or because they thought the bears might kill their livestock.

One expert on grizzly bears, Dr. John Craighead, says that the grizzly once "roamed the American West by the tens of thousands." Dr. Craighead estimates that in the western U. S. today, "probably fewer than a thousand are left."

Many grizzly bears in the United States now live in national parks. Adult grizzlies live alone. They spend most of their time searching for plants, fish, and small mammals to eat. Grizzly bears usually avoid people. But when grizzlies and people share the same area, such as in a national park, trouble can result.

Some grizzly bears in national parks once depended on scraps of food they found in park garbage dumps. These dumps were all closed by 1971. After the dumps were closed, some bears began entering campgrounds in search of food.

People have been attacked and even killed by bears searching for food. Bears that kill people are destroyed. Troublesome bears that have not seriously injured anyone may be drugged and moved to a part of the park away from people.

Federal officials are now making some areas in national parks and forests off limits to people. They hope to keep bears and humans from coming together in these places.

Park ranger in Alaska pours water on a drugged grizzly bear to cool it off. The bear developed a fever from the drug used to put it to sleep. Rangers drugged the grizzly and tied it to a stretcher so it could be safely moved to an area away from people. Grizzly bears in national parks sometimes lose their fear of humans. Such bears often enter campgrounds in search of food. The bears are moved if they become nuisances to visitors.

Protecting Forest Homelands

Grizzly cub naps while nestled on its mother. Another cub sleeps beside the mother bear. These bears live in Mt. McKinley National Park, in Alaska. Parks help protect grizzly habitats from logging and mining activities. Many wilderness areas contain valuable timber, as well as minerals, such as oil and gas. People often harvest trees and remove minerals from these wilderness areas. This sometimes creates problems for bears by bringing people into their habitats. A logger (left) saws down a giant spruce in Alaska.

Snail darter

San Francisco garter snake   Houston toad

Small Creatures Lose Their Homes

Some animals live in only one small area. If their habitats are changed, the animals may face serious problems. The habitats of the five endangered animals shown here are all different. But each habitat is being destroyed by building, draining, or farming. Four of the animals live in the United States. The snail darter is found naturally in only one part of the Little Tennessee River. The San Francisco garter snake lives in lakes and marshes around San Francisco. Central and southeast Texas is the home of the Houston toad. The Texas blind salamander lives in just one county in Texas. The fifth animal, the radiated tortoise, lives only on the southern coast of Madagascar, an island near Africa.

Texas blind salamander

Radiated tortoise

Workers finish constructing a new dam (opposite page). Later, water will form a lake behind the dam. Such dams can destroy the habitats of animals that live in a river or along its banks. A dam in Tennessee destroyed the home of small fish called snail darters. The fish were moved to another river. Experts are not sure if they will survive in their new location.

Wildlife and Domestic Animals

People can affect the habitats of animals even in the most isolated areas. For example, in the Rocky Mountains of the western United States and Canada, bighorn sheep sometimes have to share their feeding grounds with domestic sheep.

In summer, the bighorn sheep climb high into the mountains in search of food. They graze in areas where domestic animals seldom go. In winter, when these areas are covered with snow, the bighorns migrate down the mountainsides into the valleys. Often, the bighorns find that the grass in the valleys has already been eaten by domestic sheep. Ranchers take their sheep into the valleys to graze during the summer. Many times, there isn't enough grass left for the bighorns to eat during the winter.

Other problems can result when domestic animals and wild animals use the same feeding areas. Bighorns sometimes catch diseases by eating grass in areas where sick domestic sheep have grazed.

Once, there were an estimated two million bighorns. There are only about 120,000 left. Wildlife experts are trying to help bighorns by providing protected areas where the animals can find enough food.

Baby bighorn (above) in the Canadian Rockies has already sprouted its horns. An adult bighorn (right) perches on a narrow ledge in Montana.

Rocky Mountain bighorn sheep (left) stand on the heights as a rancher drives his domestic sheep down the mountainside. In winter, the bighorns will come down to graze in the area the sheep are leaving. But the domestic sheep may have eaten all the grass. If so, some of the bighorns could starve.

38

Houses and streets nearly cover a coastal area in Delaware (below). At one time, such coastal areas provided homes for a variety of animals. Loggerhead turtles once dug their nests on many Atlantic beaches. Because of housing developments, loggerhead nesting sites are becoming rare. The turtles are disturbed by bright lights and human activity.

Wildlife officials and a helper dig a new hole for loggerhead turtle eggs on a North Carolina beach (left). The men found the eggs uncovered on the sand. They had been washed from their nest by heavy waves.

Turtle eggs are carefully placed in their new nest (right). The eggs will be covered with sand to protect them until they hatch.

Nowhere To Go

When large numbers of people move into an animal's territory, the animal's problems can be enormous. This has happened to many kinds of sea turtles. There are seven species of sea turtles throughout the world. Six of these species are either threatened or endangered. One reason the turtles have suffered is that thousands of people have built homes near beaches where the turtles lay their eggs.

For millions of years, sea turtles have returned to the same beaches where they hatched. There, the turtles use their large flippers to scoop out nests in the sand. The turtles lay their eggs, cover them with sand, then return to the sea.

When the baby turtles hatch, they scurry across the sand and into the water to begin their lives at sea. Later, they too will return to the beaches where they hatched to dig nests and lay their eggs.

This ancient cycle of life is broken when people build houses near beaches used by sea turtles. Humans also break the cycle by digging up turtle eggs for food. And turtle feeding grounds on the ocean floor have been destroyed by boats dragging huge nets to catch shrimps. These problems have driven some kinds of sea turtles nearly to extinction.

The most endangered kind of sea turtle is the Kemp's ridley. The Kemp's ridley is the smallest sea turtle. It weighs about 100 pounds (45 kg). The only nesting site the Kemp's ridley has left is one beach on the east coast of Mexico.

About 25 years ago, as many as 40,000 Kemp's ridleys came to this beach each year to lay their eggs. Now, only a few 41 hundred return. The governments of Mexico and the United States are trying to start a second nesting area on Padre Island, in Texas. Kemp's ridleys nested there long ago.

People are working to save other kinds of sea turtles. Until recently, Jennifer Picker, 11, of Newark, Delaware, lived in North Carolina. There, Jennifer's father, a scientist, helped study sea turtles called loggerheads. Jennifer learned about the loggerheads' problems from her father. She wanted to help save the turtles.

Jennifer and a group of wildlife experts captured baby loggerhead turtles that might otherwise have died. They kept the baby turtles in an aquarium until they were big enough to be set free. Then they took the turtles to the ocean and released them.

"I liked working with loggerheads," said Jennifer. "If people have destroyed an animal's home, then people should try to help the animal survive."

Loggerhead turtles, such as the one below, travel up to 1,000 miles (1,600 km) yearly between nesting and feeding sites.

Jennifer Picker, 11, and fisheries expert Hughes Tillett release a baby loggerhead in the ocean off the coast of North Carolina (above). Jennifer studied and helped raise loggerheads that hatched too late in the summer to survive on their own. At right, she feeds a baby turtle. At left, she puts a turtle in a container for the trip to the ocean.

3
Wildlife For Sale

Skins of endangered jaguars hang on display at a trading post in Colombia, South America. Inside, a dealer buys more skins from a hunter. Colombia has now banned such trade.

Somewhere in the hot, shadowy rain forest of South America, a hunter searches for game. He pauses for a moment and listens carefully. Suddenly, he sees a large, spotted cat moving quietly beneath the trees.

The hunter slowly lifts his rifle and takes careful aim. He fires one shot, and the animal drops. The hunter runs toward the fallen animal. This may be his luckiest day of the year. He has killed a jaguar!

The hunter has also killed an endangered animal. He may not care that jaguars are endangered. Even though his country forbids jaguar hunting, he ignores the law. All he thinks about is the money he will make. He is a farmer with

44

Temporarily left by itself, a fuzzy 6-week-old jaguar kitten cries out. Jaguars were once common in North, Central, and South America. Some lived as far north as the southern United States. Now, they are gone from most of these areas. Thousands have been killed by hunters.

Young marchers in Washington, D. C., carry signs near the Canadian Embassy to protest the killing of harp seals. Canada allows hunters to kill about 180,000 harp seals each year.

Mother harp seal lies near her baby on the ice off Canada's southeastern coast (right). Most of the harp seals killed are pups. Canadian hunters earn a total of more than five million dollars annually from the harp seal hunt.

very little income. He will probably sell the jaguar fur for several hundred dollars—more money than he would earn in months of farming.

Jaguars once lived in many parts of North, Central, and South America. They have nearly disappeared from North America, and they have become rare in most parts of Central and South America. Hunters are partly to blame for this.

The fur of jaguars and other rare animals becomes more valuable as the animals become fewer in number. Many countries have passed laws that forbid the hunting of these animals. But hunters still kill them illegally. And sometimes, countries simply do not enforce their laws.

Laws that protect wildlife vary greatly from one nation to another. A dealer who buys the skin of an endangered animal may be able to ship the skin out of his country legally. But the country he is shipping it to may have laws forbidding trade in the skin of that animal. If that is so, the dealer will have to smuggle the skin past inspectors.

The skin may be bought and sold several times. It may eventually be added to several other skins of the same kind of animal. The skins may be made into a fur coat worth thousands of dollars.

Legal Hunting

In some countries, it is legal to hunt animals that other nations want to protect. The hunting of harp seals, for example, is allowed by Canada and Norway. And the sale of harp seal fur is legal in many other countries. But the fur of harp seals cannot legally be brought into the United States.

Harp seals migrate from the Arctic Ocean during February or March each year. They gather off Canada's southeastern coast and in the Gulf of St. Lawrence. There, they give birth to their pups.

The pups, called whitecoats, are covered with soft, white fur. By the time they are about 3 weeks old, they begin to grow gray adult coats. The pups remain on the ice where they were born until their fur changes.

While the pups are on the ice, ships bring hunters into the area. The hunters walk across the ice and kill the seals with clubs. Most of those killed are whitecoats. Their skins are shipped to Norway. There they (Continued on page 50) 47

Hunters club northern fur seals in the Pribilof Islands of Alaska. This hunt is similar to, but smaller than, the harp seal hunt. The U. S. allows about 30,000 northern fur seals to be killed here yearly. Only males without mates may be killed legally.

White-Furred Baby

Newborn harp seal, called a whitecoat, gazes at its icy world through large, dark eyes. At birth, the pups have very little fat, or blubber, to insulate them from cold water. They live on the ice for about a month, until they have grown thick layers of blubber and coarse gray coats. After that, the seals are able to survive in the icy water.

48

(Continued from page 47) are used in making things such as trimming for hats and coats. Some are even used to make stuffed toys that look like baby harp seals.

Several animal-protection groups think too many harp seals are being killed. They believe the number of seals is growing smaller. They also say that clubbing can be a cruel way to kill the seals if it is not done correctly.

Officials in countries that allow harp seal hunting say the seals are not in danger. They claim that clubbing is the quickest and least painful way to kill the animals. They also say harp seal hunting is needed to help some people earn a living.

Products From Rare Animals

While animals such as jaguars and seals are hunted for their fur, other animals are hunted for their horns, their meat, or for other parts of their bodies. People use animals in making such things as clothing, furniture, rugs, (Continued on page 55)

Animal skulls and horns lie in a heap in Kenya, Africa. Each year, thousands of Africa's animals are killed by hunters. Many are killed illegally.

Craftsmen in Kenya stuff leopards and other animals. These animals were legally killed as trophies by licensed hunters. Kenya today has outlawed such hunting. Shops like the one above have closed. Many people now visit Kenya to see living animals in their natural surroundings.

Black rhinoceros (left) in Africa faces an uncertain future. Although laws protect rhinos, some hunters kill the animals for their horns. Thousands of rhinos have been killed in Africa in the last ten years. Some experts say black rhinos may become extinct within a few years.

African elephant (below) faces problems similar to those of the rhino. Hunters often kill the elephants illegally for their tusks.

Watchful Trio

Two young Bengal tigers peer from their hiding place in the Kanha Reserve, in India. A third tiger is barely visible in the background at left. India has set aside nine such reserves. In these areas, tigers and other animals are protected from illegal hunting. Tiger hunting was banned in India in 1970. Before then, hunters killed thousands of the animals for their fur and as trophies.

53

Expensive Items from Rare Animals

Rare animals are often used to make unusual and expensive products. A few such products are shown here. Killing endangered animals to make these items is not necessary. Similar items usually can be made from other materials. Many countries have laws that forbid the shipping of anything made from rare animals. But the laws are hard to enforce. The risk of a fine or a jail sentence does not stop smugglers. One shipment of illegal furs may be worth a million dollars. The fine for shipping the furs may be only a few thousand dollars. Smugglers continue to break the law because there is a demand for illegal products.

1. Harp-seal doll; 2. Tortoiseshell jewelry; 3. Leopard-skin coat; 4. Ivory carving; 5. Dagger with rhino-horn handle; 6. Carved ivory tusk; 7. Perfume made with substance from whale; 8. Vicuña-wool cloth; 9. Elephant-skin boot; 10. Alligator-hide purse; 11. Elephant-foot umbrella stand; 12. Cheetah-skin wall hanging; 13. Polar-bear rug; 14. Sea-turtle soup.

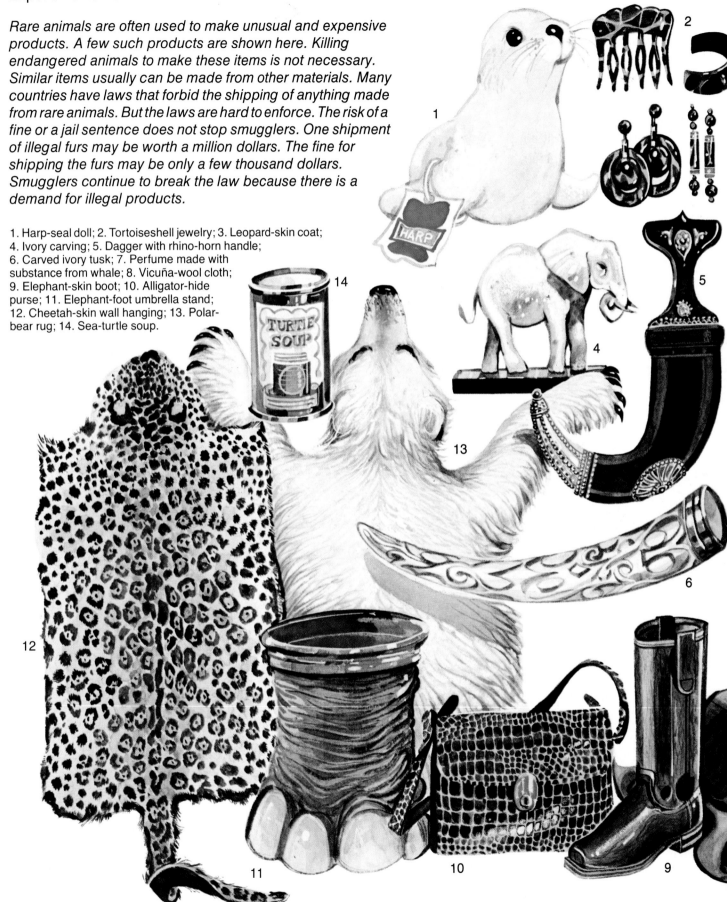

3

7

8

(Continued from page 50) perfume, and trinkets. Sometimes, only a small part of an animal is used. People who deal in things made from rare animals often make large amounts of money. Such things usually sell for high prices.

Hunters called poachers often kill animals illegally for parts of their bodies. In Africa, the black rhinoceros is nearing extinction because of illegal hunting. In the past ten years, poachers have reduced the number of black rhinos from about 20,000 to less than 2,000.

Kenya and certain other countries in Africa have banned the killing of rhinos. But poachers still kill the huge animals for their horns. Rhino horns sell for more than $300 per pound ($660 per kg) in some countries. They are used in making powders that some people believe have special powers.

The horns are used in other ways, too. In Yemen, a country in the Middle East, many men own daggers that have handles made from rhino horns. The men wear the daggers as part of their traditional dress.

The African elephant is another animal that is often killed illegally. Many elephants are killed just for their ivory tusks. The ivory is used in making chess sets, jewelry, and other items. Some people buy elephant tusks and store them. They expect the price of ivory to go higher in the future. If it does, they can sell the tusks at a profit.

It is sometimes possible to tell if an object has been made from an animal. But it is often impossible to tell what kind of animal. Some people buy objects without realizing they have been made from illegally killed endangered wildlife.

Trade in Live Animals

Just as people worldwide make large amounts of money by buying and selling things made from wild animals, people also make huge profits dealing in live animals. One expert estimates that trade in live animals amounts to tens of millions of dollars a year. Some animal collectors are willing to pay hundreds, or even thousands, of dollars each for certain kinds of rare birds.

The size of the live-animal trade can be seen in the number of animals shipped to the United States. Every year, *several million* live animals are shipped to the United States from all parts of the world. These animals include millions of fish, 55

Wild rhesus monkeys climb over stone carvings near a home in Jaipur, India. India once exported thousands of rhesus monkeys every year. After their numbers dropped sharply, India banned their export.

Researcher in Florida wears a mask to prevent the spread of germs to a rhesus monkey. Rhesus monkeys are now bred in the U. S. for use in research. Scientists have learned new facts about the human body by studying rhesus monkeys.

Crates of Asian songbirds called munias (say MEW-nee-ahs) await shipment at a warehouse in India (left). The birds have been sprayed with pink and green dye to make them more colorful for buyers in Europe and Asia. About one out of every three munia birds dies after being sprayed. Birds make up a large part of the live-animal trade. Some rare birds, such as certain kinds of parrots, sell for thousands of dollars each.

reptiles, and amphibians, hundreds of thousands of birds, and thousands of mammals.

Most of the animals shipped to the United States enter the country legally. These include some threatened or endangered animals that are imported by zoos or scientific researchers. But as many as 25 percent of the animals shipped to the U. S. each year are threatened or endangered animals that are brought into the country illegally.

To get the animals past inspectors, smugglers often use false export or import permits. They also bring in large numbers of animals by hiding them in various ways. One way they do this is to put the animals beneath false bottoms inside shipping crates containing legal merchandise.

Animals brought into the U. S. often go to pet shops. But many of the animals die before they ever reach a pet store. Some are killed when trappers try to capture them. Others die in shipment. Smugglers are more interested in selling animals than in caring for them.

For example, birds are often captured as babies. Trappers 57 sometimes catch them by cutting down trees that hold their nests. Many birds are killed this way. Those that survive may have their beaks taped shut and be hidden in the door panels or under the seats of cars entering a country.

The greatest danger to animals being smuggled is that too many of them may be placed in one container. Some may die from overcrowding. If a delay in shipping occurs, animals may starve to death. Sometimes animals die because the temperature inside their container becomes too high. This can easily happen if the animals are crowded together.

Not all live animals that people buy are kept as pets. Scientists have used animals for years in medical and other kinds of research. Rhesus monkeys, for example, were used in the development of polio vaccine. And rhesus monkeys were among the first animals to travel into space. By studying the monkeys while they were in flight and after they returned to earth, scientists learned about some of the effects that space travel might have on humans.

In the past, only about one out of every five captured monkeys ever reached a research laboratory. Most of the animals died in shipment. In the 1950s, India exported as many as 200,000 rhesus monkeys a year. But the number of monkeys in that country dropped from many millions to about one million. India stopped exporting the monkeys in 1978.

Stopping Rare-Animal Trade

People in many countries want to stop the wasteful killing of threatened and endangered wildlife. They also want to end live trade in such animals. In 1973, representatives from 87 countries met to discuss these problems. Most of the countries agreed to control the shipping of many live animals as well as products made from these animals.

Other countries around the world have not accepted this group's ideas. Even in countries that agree with the ideas, laws are often hard to enforce. Many times there are not enough officials to inspect all the shipments of animals coming into or leaving a country.

The United States, for example, has strict laws against the importation of certain animals and animal products. But in 1973, at Kennedy International Airport in New York, officials discovered a ring of fur *(Continued on page 62)*

58

Shaggy mountain goat climbs a cliff. Hunters often seek goat horns and heads as trophies.

Mountain goat surveys its home in Glacier National Park, in Montana. Laws in the western states where mountain goats live help protect the animals from overhunting.

Graceful Water Bird

Roseate spoonbill soars on outstretched wings (left). These colorful water birds live on lakes and in marshes (above) from the southern United States to Argentina, in South America. Thousands were once killed for their feathers and skins. These were used in making women's clothing at the turn of the century. Laws passed in the U. S. and other countries helped save the birds from extinction.

Egret chicks peer from their nest in Louisiana's Atchafalaya Swamp. Later, the chicks grow long, beautiful feathers.

(Continued from page 58) smugglers. Over a period of a year and a half, the smugglers bought and sold more than 99,000 animal skins worth about five million dollars. All of these skins were from threatened or endangered animals.

Some efforts to end trade in animal products have been successful. In the late 1800s, women in Europe and the United States wore hats and dresses decorated with feathers. Among the most popular feathers were those of water birds, such as spoonbills and egrets.

These fashions were so popular that feathers became an important part of the trade between some countries. Millions of birds were killed each year to meet the huge demand. So many were slaughtered that egrets and other birds were nearing extinction.

Finally, people became alarmed at the great numbers of birds being killed. Because of this concern, the United States and Great Britain passed laws in the early 1900s to stop the feather trade and protect the birds.

Since that time, spoonbills, egrets, and other birds once hunted for their feathers have increased in number. Today, flocks of these birds can still be seen in marshes and along seacoasts—all because people acted before it was too late.

62

Drawings like the one above, done in 1899, helped make people aware that millions of water birds were being killed for their feathers. The feathers were used to decorate hats and dresses. In this drawing, the artist included an egret—one of the birds often killed.

Adult egret (right) grooms its feathers in a Florida marsh. People helped save egrets from extinction by demanding an end to the hunting of the birds. Laws passed in the early 1900s protected egrets and banned the sale of their feathers. Since then, the number of egrets has greatly increased.

Covered with sticky, black oil, a western grebe sits helpless on a beach near San Francisco, California. Two tankers collided nearby, spilling tons of oil into the water. Many animals suffer because of such accidental pollution. Others are harmed by poisons introduced into their environments on purpose.

4
Deadly Substances

Volunteers use cotton swabs to clean oil from the eyes and beak of a grebe caught in an oil spill. Despite the cleaning and the weeks of care they receive, few oil-soaked birds survive.

On a dark winter night, heavy fog covers the coast of California near a busy shipping port. Two huge tankers loaded with oil move toward the narrow entrance to the port. Hidden from each other in the fog, the ships are moving on a collision course.

Suddenly, the tankers ram together in the blackness! Tons of dark, thick oil begin spilling into the water from a hole ripped in the side of one of the ships.

The oil spreads into a wide pool on the surface of the ocean. With the incoming tide, the pool of oil drifts toward the nearby shores, where thousands of water birds have come to spend the winter.

At dawn, a water bird called a western grebe takes off and flies out over the sea. It lands on the water and dives below the 65

waves. As the bird searches for fish, it swims under the floating pool of oil. When it surfaces, its feathers are coated by the sticky, black substance.

Because of the oil, the bird's feathers are no longer waterproof. Cold water begins to soak through its feathers and chill the bird. The grebe cannot escape from the polluted water because it can no longer fly. It tries to clean itself with its beak and swallows some of the poisonous oil. Without help, the grebe will soon die.

This bird is one of hundreds of thousands that have been affected by oil spills around the world. Because people today are using more oil than ever before, ships are carrying large amounts of oil from places where it is produced to places where it is needed. This constant movement of oil greatly increases the chance of accidental spills.

From 1972 to 1979, an average of 36 major oil spills occurred each year as a result of accidents involving tankers. When oil from a spill washes ashore, hundreds of people often rush to the polluted area to help clean the land and water.

These people may also try to save oil-soaked birds by cleaning them and caring for them. Usually, only a few birds survive. Most of them die from exposure to cold water or from swallowing oil.

Tankers involved in accidents dump about 225,000 tons (200,000 t) of oil into the world's oceans each year. Besides killing thousands of animals, this oil pollutes the homes of countless others.

Some kinds of animals are so few in number that an oil spill could wipe out a large part of the species. This is the case with the California sea otter.

Once, there were at least 15,000 California sea otters. The animals were nearly driven to extinction by fur hunters in the 18th and 19th centuries. After the state banned sea otter

California sea otter floats on its back in a bed of seaweed. The playful otters often wrap themselves in seaweed. This keeps them from drifting. Thousands of California sea otters were once killed by fur hunters. Though laws now protect them from hunting, the otters face a new threat. Oil spills near their
homes could kill large numbers of them.

Airplanes spray crops with the pesticide DDT. This pesticide was once used in the U. S. to kill harmful insects. But it also harmed some birds, such as pelicans. Rains washed the DDT into streams and lakes. There, it was absorbed by fish. Pelicans that ate these fish often laid eggs with shells too thin to hatch.

hunting in 1913, the number of otters slowly began to grow.

But even today, there are only about 2,000 of the animals. The otters live along the California coast between Santa Barbara and San Francisco. This happens to be an area where many oil tankers travel. An accident here could be deadly for sea otters. Experts say that a single oil spill could kill hundreds of the animals.

Polluted Habitats

Substances other than oil pollute the places where animals live. Farmers often spray their crops with chemicals called pesticides. These chemicals are sometimes needed to kill harmful insects and help farmers raise more food for the growing human population. But at times, a pesticide that has been used for years is found to be harmful to many kinds of animals. This was the case with the pesticide called DDT.

DDT was used for more than 20 years before scientists discovered that it produced harmful effects in pelicans and

Adult brown pelicans care for their young in a South Carolina refuge. The number of pelicans has begun to increase since the use of DDT was banned in the United States in 1972. 69

other birds. By 1972, officials in the United States realized how dangerous DDT could be. At that time, the federal government banned the use of the pesticide in this country. But scientists discovered that DDT does not simply disappear from the environment after it is used. Its effects can last for years, poisoning animals both in the sea and on the land.

DDT has been introduced into the environment in ways other than through its use on crops. Until 1971, a factory in California dumped chemical wastes containing DDT into the county sewer system. The wastes spread into coastal waters.

The DDT in the wastes was absorbed by tiny plants and animals living in the water. Fish that ate the plants or animals containing DDT absorbed the chemical into their own bodies. Later, brown pelicans ate the poisoned fish and were themselves poisoned.

The tiny plants and animals in the water, along with the fish that feed on them and the pelicans that eat the fish, make up what is called a food chain. In most food chains, larger animals prey on smaller ones. Because pelicans are the last members of their food chain, they received large amounts of the poison absorbed by other members of the chain.

This poison caused the pelicans to lay eggs with shells thinner than normal. Some of these eggs cracked soon after being laid. Others were crushed when adult birds sat on them to keep them warm. As a result, fewer pelicans hatched.

Thousands of brown pelicans once searched for fish in California's coastal waters. Because of DDT, the number

Scientist feeds (above, left) and weighs (above) peregrine falcon chicks. Pesticides have caused some peregrines to lay eggs that fail to hatch. To help increase the number of peregrines, scientists now breed the birds in captivity. Adult birds, such as the one below, care for the captive-bred chicks until they are old enough to be introduced into the wild.

Golden eagle chicks (above) wait for their parents to return with food. Once common in countries north of the equator, golden eagles have disappeared from many areas. Some ranchers poison the eagles because the birds sometimes kill their sheep.

Spanish imperial eagle (left) brings food to its young. The Spanish imperial eagle is one of Europe's rarest birds. Only about one hundred still live in Spain and Portugal. The eagles sometimes die from eating poisoned bait set out for other animals.

71

Pollution Everywhere

Sleeping polar bear cub nestles between its mother's paws (above). Animals all over the world are being affected by chemicals in their environments. Winds carry many chemicals around the globe. Ocean currents and migrating fish also spread poisons. The bodies of animals that live in remote parts of the world, such as polar bears in the Arctic and Adélie penguins in Antarctica (right), have been found to contain poisons. Scientists continue to make discoveries about the dangers chemicals hold for wildlife. Some poisons have been found to be more deadly and to last longer than DDT.

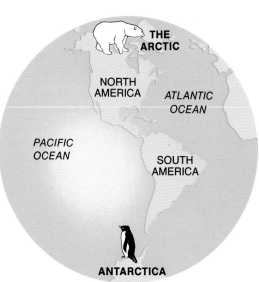

THE ARCTIC

NORTH AMERICA

ATLANTIC OCEAN

PACIFIC OCEAN

SOUTH AMERICA

ANTARCTICA

of pelicans in the state dropped from about 2,500 to 500.

Other kinds of birds have been affected by pesticides such as DDT. Because of these pesticides, some endangered birds, such as peregrine falcons, are having trouble producing enough young to keep their species alive.

Help From Humans

Peregrine falcons were once found throughout most of the United States. By 1964, the birds had disappeared from the eastern U. S. And their numbers had declined in other areas of the country. At that time, experts were able to find only about a hundred pairs of nesting peregrines in all the states except Alaska and Hawaii.

But people have found ways to help the peregrines. In 1970, scientists at Cornell University, in Ithaca, New York, began to breed peregrines in captivity. The birds' eggs are hatched in incubators. This helps increase the number of chicks produced and gives them a better chance of survival.

A week after the eggs hatch, the chicks are put with adult birds. The adult birds raise the chicks as their own. When the young peregrines are about 4 weeks old, they are taken into the wild. There, humans supply them with food while the birds learn to fly and to catch prey. In a few weeks, the young peregrines are able to survive on their own.

The people involved in this program raised and released 100 peregrines in 1979. They hope that within a few years, they will be able to raise and release up to 250 birds annually.

Young black-tailed prairie dog in South Dakota watches for danger near the entrance to its burrow.

Poison And The Prairie

Black-tailed prairie dogs are among the most numerous of the animals on North America's prairies. Some ranchers consider prairie dogs to be pests. The animals often compete with cattle and sheep for grass. In the painting below, a man puts poisoned grain near a prairie dog burrow. Although poisoning such as this has killed millions of black-tailed prairie dogs, many of the animals remain. Other animals, including black-footed ferrets (bottom), often make their homes in prairie dog

burrows. Scientists say the black-footed ferret has always been one of the rarest American mammals. Ferrets depend on prairie dogs as their main food source. Some experts believe the killing of large numbers of prairie dogs in the past may have caused a decline in the number of black-footed ferrets.

Underground Dwellers *Burrowing owls stand near their home. These long-legged*

birds are also called prairie dog owls because they often make their homes in empty prairie dog burrows.

War Against Coyotes

Many ranchers on the prairies believe the coyote is a pest. They say coyotes sometimes kill their sheep, chickens, and calves. People destroy nearly 400,000 coyotes each year. Once, many of the animals were poisoned. But other kinds of animals were sometimes accidentally killed by poisons set out for coyotes.

In 1972, most poisons used to kill coyotes were banned by the federal government on public lands. Today, people usually trap or shoot the animals. The Montana ranchers in the picture above hunt coyotes from an airplane. A coyote they have shot hangs from the side of the plane. The ranchers will sell the animal's pelt to a fur dealer. A coyote pup (right) hides in tall grass. Many wildlife experts say the coyote plays a useful role in maintaining the balance of nature. In spite of the large number of coyotes killed each year, the animals are expanding their range. They now live in some eastern states where they were not found before.

Bison calves in Montana rest near adult members of the herd. The bison was driven nearly to extinction in the late 1800s. It was saved after laws were passed to protect it. Many people worked to keep the bison from becoming extinct, just as people today are working to save other kinds of animals.

5
A Future For Some

Herd of bison blocks a train's path in this painting done in the 1800s. Before the bison became endangered, such scenes were common on the prairies of the western United States.

It is a summer day in the 1870s. A hot wind blows across a wide, flat prairie in the American West. Thousands of bison, or American buffalo, cover the broad plain. Some lie dozing in the sun. Others graze on the rich grass. Now and then, one of the bison lifts its huge head and blinks at two gleaming bands of steel that run across the prairie. These are the shiny new tracks of a railroad.

Far in the distance, a train appears. The bison hear the chug of the train's engine. They turn their heads and watch as the train draws nearer.

Suddenly, men leaning from windows on the train begin to point excitedly at the herd. "Quick," the men shout, "get your rifles!"

Hundreds of shots ring out, blending with the noise of the train. It is several seconds before the bison sense danger. As members of the herd bellow an alarm, the terrified animals stampede away from the train. For many of the animals, the 81 alarm has come too late. Nearly a thousand bison have been killed. But these animals were not killed for food or for their hides. The men aboard the train shot the bison only to amuse themselves on their long ride across the prairie.

During the 1800s, people often shot bison this way. Some railroads even advertised the fact that their trains traveled through areas where the animals could be shot from cars.

At that time, millions of bison roamed the western United States and Canada. People thought the animals would always be plentiful. Because of this belief, people nearly caused the bison to become extinct.

Saving the Bison

When European settlers first arrived in North America, bison were probably more numerous than any other large land animal in the world. Experts say there may have been 60 million bison in what is now the United States. Early travelers reported seeing herds so dense they "blackened the country."

Millions of bison were killed for sport or for food. Countless others were slaughtered for their hides. In just one year, 1873, nearly a million bison hides were shipped to fur markets in the East.

People killed so many of the animals that by the late 1800s, only one tiny herd of wild bison was left in the entire

Bison rest and graze in Yellowstone National Park, in Wyoming (above). In the background, steam rises from springs of hot water called geysers. Yellowstone was America's first national park. In the 1890s, it provided a refuge for the last remaining wild bison, a herd of fewer than 50 animals. That herd has now grown in number to 1,500. Bison, such as the one at right, are America's largest land animals. Males stand as tall as six feet (185 cm) at the shoulder and may weigh 2,000 pounds (900 kg).

Two male elk (left) battle in the National Elk Refuge, in Wyoming. Thousands of elk died in the 1800s because people took over much of their habitat. Refuges such as this helped save the elk.

83

United States. That herd of a few dozen animals lived in Yellowstone National Park, in Wyoming.

Many people realized there was danger that the bison could soon become extinct. Because of this, federal and state governments passed laws in the 1890s and early 1900s to end bison hunting. Canada also passed laws to save its bison.

The small herds that were left in both countries began to grow. Now there are more than 55,000 bison in the United States and Canada.

The bison was saved from extinction because people acted before it was too late. Today, the fate of many animals depends on whether people take action in time to save them.

Helping the Greater Snow Goose

The story of the bison is an example of how much people can do to help an animal. The story of the greater snow goose is another example. In the 1800s and early 1900s, U. S. and Canadian hunters along the Atlantic coast killed thousands of greater snow geese. By 1931, only about 7,000 of these birds

Flock of greater snow geese takes flight in a wildlife refuge in North Carolina (left). Refuges and strict hunting laws helped save the greater snow goose from extinction.

Male wood duck swims in a marsh in Minnesota (right). Overhunting and habitat loss in the late 1800s nearly drove wood ducks to extinction. A 23-year hunting ban helped save this bird. There are now several million wood ducks.

were left. In that year, the United States banned the hunting of greater snow geese in this country. Refuges were created along the migration route of the geese to provide areas where the birds could rest and find food. Under this protection, the flocks of greater snow geese began to grow.

By 1975, the population of greater snow geese had increased to about 200,000. Today, people can once again hunt these birds. But the number of birds that each hunter may kill is carefully controlled.

Experts hope that with continued protection, the growing flocks of greater snow geese will spread to more parts of their former range along the Atlantic coast.

Protecting Valuable Animals

Like the bison and the snow goose, South America's vicuña (say vie-KOON-yuh) was once hunted nearly to extinction. The vicuña lives high in the Andes mountains in the countries of Chile, Bolivia, Argentina, and Peru. These animals have long been hunted for their valuable wool.

Before Europeans conquered South America in the 1500s, Indians called Incas ruled the Andes region. At that time, it was a crime punishable by death for anyone but royalty to wear cloth made of vicuña wool. The Incas rounded up vicuñas and sheared them like sheep. Then they set the animals free. Experts believe there may have been a million vicuñas at the time of the Incas.

After South America was conquered, many Europeans wanted clothes made of vicuña wool. But instead of shearing the vicuñas as the Incas had done, the Europeans killed the animals and took their hides. This was easier to do than catching and shearing them. So many vicuñas were killed over the centuries that by 1965 fewer than 10,000 were left.

In 1969, countries where the animals live banned vicuña hunting and trade in vicuña products. The countries also made efforts to protect the animal's habitat. Since then, the number of vicuñas has increased to more than 50,000.

Because of this increase, officials in Peru have made plans to start new vicuña herds in different areas. The government also plans to allow people to kill a limited number of the animals for their meat and hides. And officials hope to reintroduce the Inca method of shearing vicuñas for their wool.

Rare South American Animal

Vicuñas wander across grassy slopes high in the Andes mountains of Peru. South America's vicuñas are related to the camel. Vicuña wool is used to make a soft cloth. Over the years, millions of the animals have been killed for their wool. Vicuña wool was valued at about $90 per pound ($200 per kg) in 1979. Most vicuñas now live on private ranches and in government reserves. Protected from hunting since 1969, the vicuña is steadily increasing in number.

87

Working To Save a Predator

Dr. Maurice Hornocker fits a drugged mountain lion with a radio collar (below). The collar will help the scientist keep track of the animal in the wild. Mountain lions were once common throughout the U. S. Now only a few thousand survive. Most live in the mountains of western states. The mountain lion at right lives in Utah. Thousands of mountain lions have been killed because the cats sometimes prey on livestock, such as cattle. Experts say the mountain lion plays a valuable role in the wild. By preying on deer and elk, the cats help keep herds from becoming too large for their ranges. Some states have passed laws to limit the number of mountain lions that are killed.

Researcher examines whooping crane eggs to be put in sandhill crane nests. The sandhills will hatch the eggs and raise the chicks.

Whooper eggs are unloaded at the sandhill nesting grounds, in Idaho. The eggs come from other parts of the United States and Canada.

Scientist puts a whooping crane egg in a sandhill nest. Sandhills are helping the rare whooping crane increase in number.

Young whoopers raised by sandhills migrate with sandhill flocks. Whooping cranes migrate between Canada and Texas. The sandhills migrate between Idaho and New Mexico.

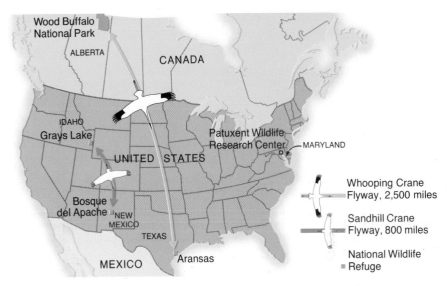

Nations Working Together

People from different countries often work together to save animals. The effort to save the vicuña is an example of this. Another example is the great effort that has been made to help North America's whooping crane. People in the United States and Canada have worked for more than 40 years to save this rare bird.

Whooping cranes were never common. There were probably no more than 4,000 of the birds at any one time. Their numbers decreased greatly in the last century because of a loss of habitat. And many of the cranes were shot by hunters as they flew on their long migrations. By 1941, only 21 whooping cranes were left.

Most of the whooping cranes lived in two refuges in the United States and Canada. One, the Aransas National Wildlife Refuge, is at the birds' winter home in Texas. The other, Wood Buffalo National Park, is at the birds' summer breeding grounds in Canada (see map above).

Over the years, biologists working to save the whooping crane have studied the birds at these refuges and at the Patuxent Wildlife Research Center, in Maryland. These

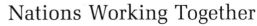

Whooping cranes, such as the pair in Texas at left, mate for life. Whoopers once ranged from New Jersey to the Rockies. 91

scientists have learned that while whoopers normally produce two chicks each year, usually only one survives.

To increase the chances that both chicks will live, the biologists began using sandhill cranes as foster parents for whooping cranes in 1975. The biologists do this by removing one of the two eggs from a whooping crane nest and putting it into a sandhill crane nest. The sandhill crane hatches the whooper egg and raises the chick as if it were its own. Scientists hope the whooping cranes raised by sandhills will breed and start their own flocks.

It may be years before scientists find out if this program is a complete success. But the program has already produced some positive results. Although the number of whoopers is still dangerously low, as of 1979 the whooping crane population had increased to 119 birds.

Whooping crane, the tall white bird on the right, strolls with sandhill cranes. The birds are at the sandhills' winter home, in New Mexico. This whooper hatched from an egg placed in a sandhill nest. Its sandhill foster parents raised the whooper as their own. The bands on the whooper's legs help scientists follow its migrations.

Biologist George Archibald studies a whooping crane named Tex at the International Crane Foundation's research center, in Wisconsin. The foundation studies 15 kinds of cranes.

George Archibald feeds birds from the foundation's captive sandhill crane flock.

Large male orangutan chews on a piece of plant. Orangutans live in Southeast Asia. Refuges and strict hunting laws now help to protect these rare animals.

Hawaii's state bird, the nene (right), was saved from extinction through breeding in captivity. Most nenes now live in refuges.

Another Chance for Wildlife

Some species of animals have become so few in number that it is nearly impossible for them to survive without human help. This is true of the whooping crane. It is also true of the red-haired ape called the orangutan. Scientists say probably only a few thousand orangutans still live in the wild. Experts believe the species will become extinct before the year 2000 unless a great amount of work is done to save it.

Orangutans live in dense rain forests on Borneo and Sumatra, islands in Southeast Asia. Many of the rain forests on these islands have been cut down. Orangutans have been driven out of other rain forests by people who hunt the animals for food or capture them to sell to animal exporters.

As part of an effort to help save the orangutan, areas are now being set aside where the apes can live in safety. And experts are now putting some of the animals back into rain forests where orangutans lived in the past.

The nene (say NAY-nay) is another animal that scientists   95

Wildlife researcher Melissa Ditton notes the behavior of a golden lion marmoset named Marmalade. The marmoset lives in a refuge for rare animals run by the National Zoo of Washington, D. C. At left, a parent and its young huddle together. The marmoset's forest habitat in Brazil has nearly disappeared. Very few of these small monkeys still live in the wild. Captive-breeding programs may be necessary to save animals such as marmosets from extinction.

Père David's deer cools itself in the water on the English estate known as Woburn Abbey. Other members of the herd graze nearby. This species of deer lives only in captivity.

are putting back into areas where it once lived. Also called the Hawaiian goose, the nene is the state bird of Hawaii. At one time, there were about 25,000 of the birds. But thousands of nenes were shot for sport. Many were killed by other animals. And livestock such as goats and pigs took over many of the birds' feeding areas. The number of nenes had dropped to fewer than 50 by 1949.

In that year, experts began breeding the birds in captivity. The experts released captive-bred birds in refuges that were set up in the nene's original mountain habitat. Since this program began, the number of nenes has grown to nearly 8,000 birds.

Other animals that are bred in captivity have few areas left in the wild where they can live. The golden lion marmoset, a long-haired South American monkey about the size of a squirrel, has lost nearly all its original habitat. Much of the marmoset's present home in Brazil has been taken over by spreading cities, farms, and ranches.

No more than 200 golden lion marmosets still live in the wild. To help save the species, the National Zoo of Washington, D. C., is breeding marmosets at its refuge for rare species in Virginia and at the zoo. With help, the golden lion marmoset may survive. But it may be able to live only in captivity.

Last Place of Refuge

In the future, many kinds of animals may be able to survive only in captivity. This is already the case with the Père David's deer—an animal that has not existed in the wild for more than 2,000 years.

This deer would be extinct today if a French missionary, Père David, had not gone to China in 1861. There, in a royal game reserve, Père David discovered a herd of these rare animals. He asked the Chinese to send some of the deer to zoos in Europe. Later, England's Duke of Bedford bought some of the deer from the zoos and started his own herd.

By 1920, all the deer in China and in the European zoos had either died or been killed. The only members of this species to survive were those belonging to the Duke of Bedford. The Père David's deer is alive today because of this series of events. Several new herds have since been started from the Duke of Bedford's herd.

97

It's Up to All of Us

People often wonder what they can do to help wild animals in their struggle to survive. Many experts say the simplest way to help is to obey laws that protect wildlife. Another way is to join groups that are working for the benefit of animals.

Some experts say that one of the most important things people can do is to take the needs of animals into consideration whenever possible. At times, this means people may have to make a small change in the way they live.

This is happening today in Santa Cruz County, in California. There, people are trying to save the rare 3-inch-long (8 cm) Santa Cruz long-toed salamander. Since 1976, this county has not allowed any construction near the salamander's home that would block the animal's migration routes or destroy its habitat. Members of the community know their actions will help determine whether the salamander survives.

People such as the residents of this county believe that an animal has a right to survive simply because it exists. They know that a living animal is more interesting than one that remains only as a museum display or as a picture in a book. They also know that when any kind of animal disappears, the entire world has lost something that can never be replaced.

Santa Cruz salamander scurries up a specially designed ramp. The California county where most of these tiny animals live forbids any building that might disturb the salamanders.

Whale-shaped balloon named Flo floats near the Lincoln Memorial in Washington, D. C. Groups such as the one that sponsors Flo are an important part of the effort to save animals.

U.S.A. FOR THE WHALES

Glossary

This book contains several words that may be new to you. Their meanings are explained below. Knowing what these words mean should help you understand this and other books you read about wildlife.

adapt—to adjust to a new condition, such as a change in environment

banned—not allowed

breed—to produce young

captivity—state of being confined, as when kept in a zoo or animal park

domestic animals—animals kept by humans, such as dogs, cats, cattle, or sheep

endangered—being reduced to the point of nearly disappearing

environment—surroundings, including air, water, land, and living things

export—to ship something out of a country

extinct—no longer in existence

foster parents—parents that raise young that are not their own

habitat—area where an animal lives naturally

import—to bring something into a country

incubator—machine used to hatch eggs or to keep young animals warm

migration—movement of animals from one place to another at certain times of the year

nesting—activities of building nests, laying eggs, and hatching chicks

overhunting—killing so many of one kind of animal that the species becomes few in number

pesticide—chemical used to get rid of a pest

poacher—person who hunts illegally

pollute—to introduce harmful substances into the environment

prey—one animal hunted by another animal for food

rain forest—tall, dense forest that grows in tropical areas having heavy annual rainfall

range—entire area over which members of a species can be found

refuge—area where animals are protected from danger

reserve—land set aside so animals can live in their natural surroundings

smuggle—to take something of value from one place to another illegally

species—all the animals of one kind that can mate and produce young like themselves

territory—area controlled by one animal or group of animals

threatened—facing serious threats to survival

wetlands—areas that have wet soil, such as marshes or swamps

Index

Bold type refers to illustrations; regular type refers to text.

COVER: *African cheetah, the world's fastest land animal, is now endangered because of hunting and habitat loss.*

Additional Reading

Readers may want to check the National Geographic Index in a school or public library for related articles, and to refer to the following books:

General books: Allen, Thomas B., *Vanishing Wildlife of North America* (National Geographic Society, 1974). Duplaix, Nicole and Simon, Noel, *World Guide to Mammals* (Crown Publishers, Inc., 1976). Leen, Nina, *And Then There Were None, America's Vanishing Wildlife* (Holt, Rinehart and Winston, 1973). McClung, Robert M., *Lost Wild America, The Story of Our Extinct and Vanishing Wildlife* (William Morrow and Company, 1969); *Lost Wild Worlds, The Story of Extinct and Vanishing Wildlife of the Eastern Hemisphere* (William Morrow and Company, 1976). McCoy, J. J., *In Defense of Animals* (Seabury Press, Inc., 1978); *Saving Our Wildlife* (Crowell-Collier Press, 1970). Stewart, Darryl, *Canadian Endangered Species* (Gage Publishing Limited/Vanguard, 1974); *From the Edge of Extinction, The Fight to Save Endangered Species* (Methuen, 1978). *Wild Animals of North America* (National Geographic Society, 1979).
Books about specific kinds of animals: Curto, Josephine, *Biography of an Alligator* (G. P. Putnam's Sons, 1976). George, Jean Craighead, *The Wounded Wolf* (Harper & Row, 1978). Graham, Ada and Graham, Frank, *Falcon Flight* (Delacorte Press, 1978). Kahl, M. P., *Wonders of Storks* (Dodd, Mead & Company, 1978). Lavine, Sigmund A. and Scuro, Vincent, *Wonders of the Bison World* (Dodd, Mead & Company, 1975). Laycock, George, *Autumn of the Eagle* (Charles Scribner's Sons, 1973). McClung, Robert M., *America's Endangered Birds, Programs and People Working to Save Them* (William Morrow and Company, 1979); *Black Jack, Last of the Big Alligators* (William Morrow and Company, 1967); *Hunted Mammals of the Sea* (William Morrow and Company, 1978). Riedman, Sarah R. and Witham, Ross, *Turtles, Extinction or Survival?* (Abelard-Schuman, 1974). Ryden, Hope, *The Little Deer of the Florida Keys* (G. P. Putnam's Sons, 1978); *The Wild Pups, The True Story of a Coyote Family* (G. P. Putnam's Sons, 1975). Scott, Jack Denton, *Little Dogs of the Prairie* (G. P. Putnam's Sons, 1977); *Loggerhead Turtle, Survivor from the Sea* (G. P. Putnam's Sons, 1974); *Return of the Buffalo* (G. P. Putnam's Sons, 1976); *That Wonderful Pelican* (G. P. Putnam's Sons, 1975). Steiner, Barbara A., *Biography of a Wolf* (G. P. Putnam's Sons, 1973).

Consultants

Nicole Duplaix, TRAFFIC(U.S.A.); Dr. Ronald M. Nowak, Office of Endangered Species, U. S. Fish and Wildlife Service, *Chief Consultants*
Dr. Glenn O. Blough, *Educational Consultant*
Dr. Nicholas J. Long, *Consulting Psychologist*

The Special Publications and School Services Division is grateful to the individuals, organizations, and agencies named or quoted in the text and to the individuals cited here for their generous assistance: Dr. George Balazs, Hawaii Institute of Marine Biology; Alice Berkner, International Bird Rescue Research Center; Tom Cade, Cornell University; California Department of Fish and Game; Dr. Archie Carr III, Florida Audubon Society; Center for Short-Lived Phenomena; Jan Nagel Clarkson; Judith M. Hobart; Dr. Maurice Hornocker, Idaho Cooperative Wildlife Research Unit; International Crane Foundation; Werner Janney; Donald J. Kosin, National Key Deer Wildlife Refuge; David Mack, TRAFFIC(U.S.A.); Dr. Shirley McGreal, International Primate Protection League; Dr. Mary Meagher, Yellowstone National Park; Anne Meylan, University of Florida; National Zoological Park, Smithsonian Institution: Dr. Theodore Reed, Dr. Devra Kleiman, John Seidensticker, Dr. Christian Wemmer; Sue Pressman and the Institute for Animal Problems, Humane Society of the United States; Dr. Frederick W. Schuierer, Cabrillo College; U. S. Fish and Wildlife Service: Dr. Ray Erickson, Conrad N. Hillman, Dr. Vivian Mendenhall, Henry M. Reeves, William W. Rightmire, Jay Sheppard, Jim Williams; Dr. George E. Watson, Smithsonian Institution.

Library of Congress CIP Data

Stuart, Gene S
   Wildlife alert!

(Books for world explorers)
Bibliography: p.   Includes index.

SUMMARY: Discusses the many problems that animals around the world face and what people are doing to help. A wall poster and a 24-page booklet of games and puzzles are included.

1. Wildlife conservation—Juvenile literature. 2. Endangered species—Juvenile literature. [1. Rare animals. 2. Wildlife conservation] I. Title. II. Series.   QL83.S78   333.95'4   79-1792   ISBN 0-87044-318-6

Composition for WILDLIFE ALERT! by National Geographic's Photographic Services, Carl M. Shrader, Chief; Lawrence F. Ludwig, Assistant Chief. Printed and bound by Holladay-Tyler Printing Corp., Rockville, Md. Color separations by the Lanman Companies, Washington, D. C.; National Bickford Graphics, Inc., Providence, R.I.; Progressive Color Corp., Rockville, Md.; The J. Wm. Reed Co., Alexandria, Va.; Holladay-Tyler Printing Corp., Rockville, Md.

Illustrations Credits

WILDLIFE ALERT!
The Struggle to Survive
by Gene S. Stuart

PUBLISHED BY
THE NATIONAL GEOGRAPHIC SOCIETY

Robert E. Doyle, *President*
Melvin M. Payne, *Chairman of the Board*
Gilbert M. Grosvenor, *Editor*
Melville Bell Grosvenor, *Editor Emeritus*

PREPARED BY THE SPECIAL PUBLICATIONS
AND SCHOOL SERVICES DIVISION

Robert L. Breeden, *Director*
Donald J. Crump, *Associate Director*
Philip B. Silcott, *Assistant Director*

STAFF FOR BOOKS FOR WORLD EXPLORERS SERIES: Ralph Gray, *Editor*; Pat Robbins, *Managing Editor*; Ursula Perrin Vosseler, *Art Director*

STAFF FOR WILDLIFE ALERT!: Paul D. Martin, *Managing Editor*; William L. Allen, *Picture Editor*; Ursula Perrin Vosseler, *Designer*; Alison Wilbur, *Assistant Picture Editor*; Eleanor Shannahan, Nancy J. Watson, *Researchers*; Karen Skeirik, *Assistant Researcher*

ILLUSTRATIONS AND DESIGN: Beth Molloy, *Design Assistant*; John D. Garst, Jr., Peter J. Balch, Lisa Biganzoli, Susanah B. Brown, Gary M. Johnson, Patricia J. King, Dorothy Michele Novick, Alfred L. Zebarth, *Map Research, Design, and Production*

FAR-OUT FUN!: Eleanor Shannahan, *Project Editor*; Nancy J. Watson, *Researcher*; Karen Skeirik, *Assistant Researcher*; Sara A. Grosvenor, *Research Assistant*

ENGRAVING, PRINTING, AND PRODUCT MANUFACTURE: Robert W. Messer, *Manager*; George V. White, *Production Manager*; Raja D. Murshed, June L. Graham, Christine A. Roberts, Richard A. McClure, *Assistant Production Managers*; David V. Showers, *Production Assistant*; Susan M. Oehler, *Staff Assistant*

STAFF ASSISTANTS: Debra A. Antonini, Pamela A. Black, Barbara Bricks, Jane H. Buxton, Mary Elizabeth Davis, Rosamund Garner, Nancy J. Harvey, Jane M. Holloway, Joan Hurst, Suzanne J. Jacobson, Artemis S. Lampathakis, Cleo Petroff, Marcia Robinson, Katheryn M. Slocum

INTERNS: Rebecca Anne Garrett, Betsy L. Grasso, Kit Pancoast, Louise Ponsford, Janet C. Poort, Cobie van L. Maas

MARKET RESEARCH: Joe Fowler, Patrick Fowler, Karen A. Geiger, Cynthia B. Lew, Meg McElligott, Stephen F. Moss

INDEX: Anne K. McCain